For Bruton Primary School
and all its hard-working staff

First published in the United Kingdom in 2001
by Ragged Bears Publishing Limited,
Milborne Wick, Sherborne, Dorset DT9 4PW

Distributed by Ragged Bears Limited, Ragged Appleshaw,
Andover, Hampshire SP11 9HX
Tel: 01264 772269

A CIP record of this book is available from the British Library
ISBN 185714 218 7 (hb)
ISBN 185714 220 9 (pb)

Printed in China

I've got nits!

MIKE BROWNLOW

Let me introduce you to
The Fotheringtons, a family who
Are Mum and Dad, their baby Benny,
And their little daughter Jenny.

Now Jenny always looked her best,
Clean and scrubbed and smartly dressed.

And Jenny, just like many girls,
Had lovely hair with lovely curls.
It gleamed and shimmered in the light
And gave her parents great delight.

Each morning when she went to school,
(Her parents took her as a rule),
Her mum and dad would smile with pride,
And feel just slightly smug inside.

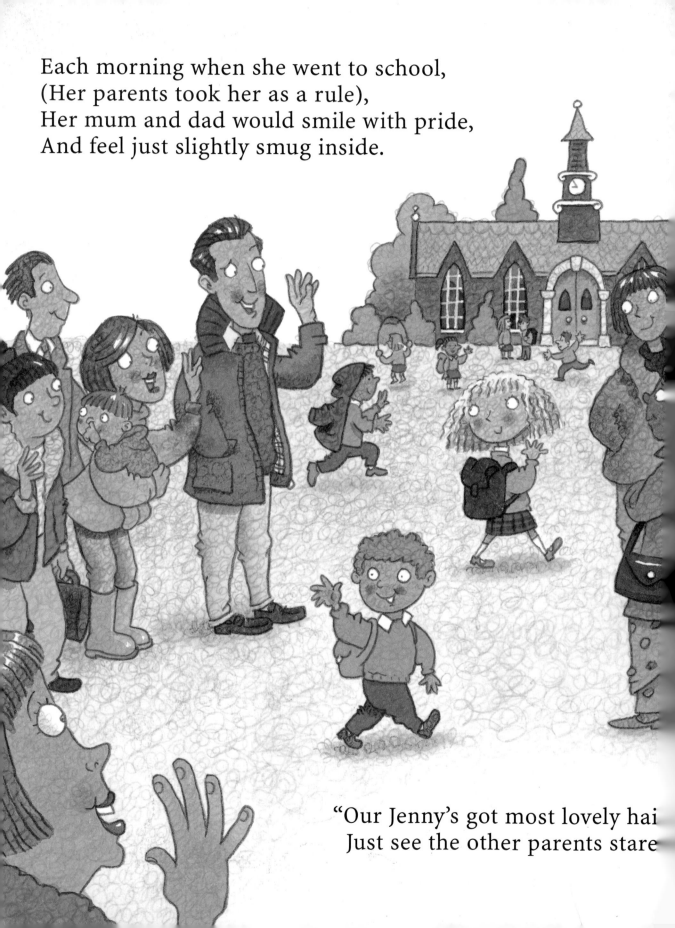

"Our Jenny's got most lovely hai
Just see the other parents stare

Her hair was washed despite the troubles,
Frequently with lots of bubbles.
And each night sitting on her bed
Her mum would brush young Jenny's head.
She'd beam with pride and brush away,
One hundred brush strokes every day.

But late one night, about to brush
Jen's mummy had a nasty flush!
She gulped and gasped and felt quite weak,
And uttered one small strangled squeak.
Her jaw dropped down, her eyebrows rose,
The blood within her body froze.

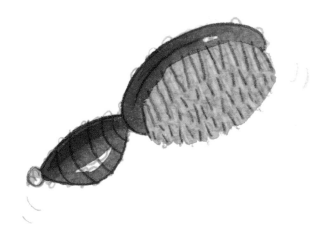

For there beneath her mother's stare.....
Something MOVED in Jenny's hair!

Jenny's mum looked horrified.
"My darling's got the nits!" she cried.
Jenny's dad came rushing in
To find the cause of all the din.
He focussed on his little girl
And magnified each golden curl.
"Yes..... head lice, nits! Oh golly gosh!
We can't have them .....we're clean and posh!"

That night young Jenny couldn't sleep,
(She'd tried but failed at counting sheep).

She thought and gave her head an itch,
"What are they like, these nasty nits?"

"Do they swing like Tarzan through
My hair..... you know I bet they do!
Or maybe they play hide and seek
And run around and shout and squeak!

And then I guess they'll probably
Build their house on top of me!
Or maybe they will have a fair
With swings and rides around my hair!"

"I think this really is the limit.....
My hair's got horrid head lice in it!"

Next day the family, seeing red,
Rushed to school to see the Head.
They just barged in..... they didn't knock,
And gave the Head a nasty shock.
"Nits!" they screamed. "Our Jenny's got 'em!"
The Head fell back upon his bottom.
"They can't infest our lovely daughter.....
There ought to be a law, there oughta!"

"We bet they came from Nancy Fud
Who's usually caked in mud.

Or maybe little Henry Platts
Whose family keep one hundred cats.

And now, oh dear,
despite our riches,
Even Baby Benny itches!"

The Head stood up and raised his arm,
He rubbed his bottom, begged for calm.
The Head he said, "Now don't feel squealy,
Head lice are quite common really.

They're teeny weeny insects which
Unfortunately make you itch.
They're everywhere..... annoyingly
We have an outbreak frequently.

They love clean hair..... oh yes they do,
That's why the nits have chosen you.

And you can catch them just like that
By sharing brushes, scarves or hats."

"Or if two heads of hair are near
For just too long, the head lice cheer.
They cry 'Yippee..... a chance to roam,
Another head to call our home!'"

With everybody scratching now,
The Fotheringtons enquired how
To rid themselves of horrid lice,
"It really isn't very nice."

The Head sat down and stroked his lip,
"I really only have one tip.....
We've tried but failed with smelly lotions;
Sadly we've no magic potions."

"Combing..... that's the thing to do.
Nice wet hair..... conditioner too.
If everyone in Jenny's class
Does the same, the nits won't last.

One final thing you need to know,
Dear Fotheringtons, before you go.....
As parents you have prob'ly got 'em.
Fine-tooth-combing..... that'll stop 'em."

They thanked the Head and with a sigh,
And one last scratch, they said goodbye.

And later on when Jen came home,
Mum washed her hair with lots of foam.
Simple shampoo, rinse and then
Conditioner was poured on Jen.

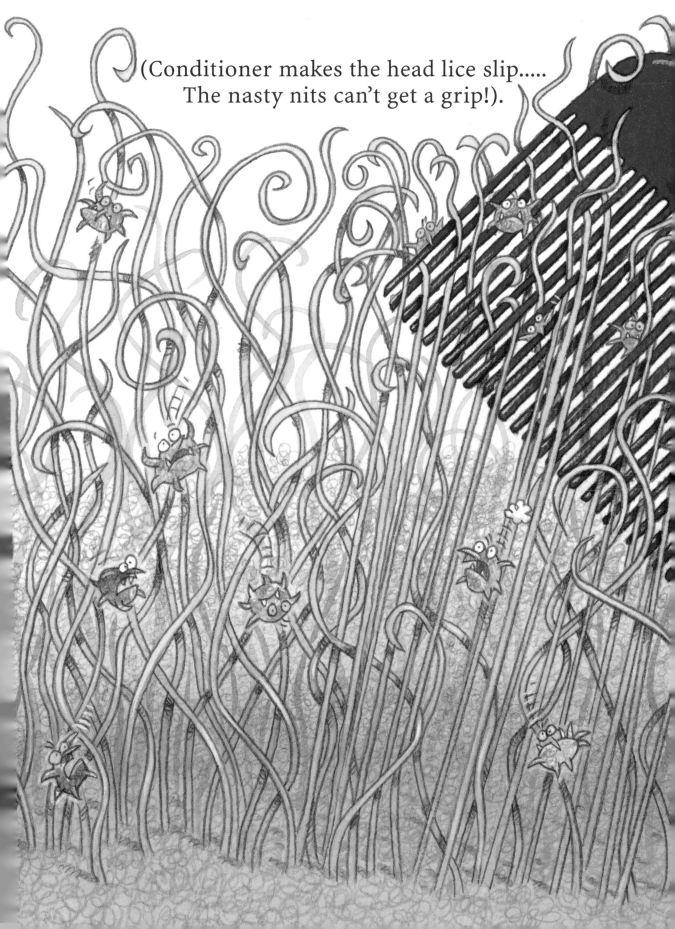

(Conditioner makes the head lice slip.....
The nasty nits can't get a grip!).

Next, before the telly's glare,
Mum fine-tooth-combed young Jenny's hair.
And then the same for Dad and Mum
And Benny while he sucked his thumb.

Three times a week they washed and brushed,
(These sort of things just can't be rushed).
But guess what? You will be amazed.....
The nits had gone in 20 days!

A Step by Step Guide to Head Lice

(Pediculus humanus capitis)

What are they?

Head lice are small insects, about 2.5mm when fully grown. They live on the scalp at the base of the hair, where they find both food and warmth. They are grey/brown in colour. Female head lice lay eggs which are glued to the base of the hair, and can be very difficult to see. The eggs are called nits, and as hair grows at the rate of approximately 1 cm a month, the nits will be seen to 'move' up the hair shaft at this rate.

Unless nits are removed by hand, they will stay stuck to the hair until they grow out. It takes between 6 to 9 days for the nits (eggs) to hatch. The egg hatches releasing a nymph, or baby head louse, which will be about the size of a pinhead. It takes about 7 - 14 days for a nymph to develop into an adult and be able to mate. The empty egg cases are yellow or white and shiny in colour.

LOUSE   **EGG**

What do head lice feed on?

Head lice are parasites. That means they live on the 'host', or the person whose hair they have infested. They feed on blood by biting through the host's scalp. The saliva of head lice can cause reactions such as severe itching and irritation leading to rashes on the scalp and down the nape of the neck.

How do you catch head lice?

They move by crawling through the hair - they cannot jump, swim or fly. You catch head lice by personal head-to-head contact: it is not so common to catch lice from bedding, hats or combs as head lice cannot live very long away from the warmth and security of a host, however it does happen and therefore this possibility should not be ignored. Head lice do not infect animals, but adult human beings can catch them as well. Head lice can affect clean or dirty hair.

How do you know if you've got head lice?

There are three main ways to find out:

1 By using a very fine-tooth-comb you may be able to comb lice and empty egg-cases out of your hair. If you do this over a piece of white paper, they will be easier to spot;
2 Wash your hair in the usual way, but use plenty of conditioner, and before you wash the conditioner off, comb your hair with a special nit comb;
3 Ask someone to search your hair for nits, which will be firmly stuck to your hair.

How can you treat them?

The best way to control head lice is to check hair every week.
There are two ways of getting rid of head lice.

1 Wet-combing method. This is safe, cheap and works well. All you need is a large bottle of hair conditioner, a nit comb, and time and patience. Wash your hair as normal, then apply plenty of hair conditioner. Comb your hair with a fine nit comb, combing from the roots upwards. Check the comb for lice, and clear them away after each sweep. Comb all your hair, a little at a time, carefully, paying particular attention to the areas that lice seem to like the best; behind the ears and the back of the head down the nape of the neck. Repeat this every 3 days for 2 weeks. Remember to check everyone in the family.

   Adding essential oils such as tea tree or rosemary oil to conditioner (10 drops of oil to 100ml of conditioner) is thought to act as a good repellent to head lice, but these oils are very strong and should <u>never</u> be applied 'neat' to the scalp, or any other part of the body, only diluted in conditioner or shampoo.

2 You can buy a variety of lice-killing lotions or shampoos from the pharmacist. However, it is strongly recommended that you use the wet-combing method rather than the chemical lotions. Chemicals do not always work, lice can become resistant to them, and the continued use of these chemicals may be harmful to your health.

For further information on head lice, contact your local health authority or local surgery practice nurse.